UNSTOPPABLE

LET GO, IT WILL ALL WORK OUT

I BOOKY

Table of Contents

CHAPTER 1

THE ART OF SURRENDER

Introduction

In the high-stakes world of personal growth, we are often taught that success hinges on maintaining an iron grip on every aspect of our lives. But what if the key to true power and liberation lies not in control, but in surrender? Welcome to Chapter 1: "The Art of Surrender."

In these pages, we delve into the art of relinquishing control and embracing the transformative beauty of surrender. Prepare to uncover a profound paradigm shift—one that challenges conventional notions and propels you toward greater clarity, resilience, and success.

Get ready to unlock the hidden potential that awaits when you release the reins and trust in the wisdom of letting go. Join us as we navigate the uncharted territory of vulnerability, leading you to discover the unparalleled strength found in the surrender of self.

In this chapter, we unravel the secrets of surrender, illuminating the path to enhanced decision-making, enriched relationships, and ultimately, a more fulfilling journey. The art of surrender is not a sign of weakness; it is a testament to the courage and wisdom required to embrace life's unpredictable twists.

Welcome to a journey that will forever transform your perspective. Are you ready to master the art of surrender and unlock the power that awaits?

Let's embark on this captivating exploration together.

THE MEANING OF SURRENDER

Surrender is a concept that carries multifaceted meanings, transcending its conventional associations with defeat and weakness. At its core, surrender involves voluntarily letting go of the need to control outcomes, circumstances, or other people.

It is a conscious act of releasing the grip on the steering wheel of life and accepting the flow of events without resistance. Surrender goes beyond resignation; it is an empowered choice to embrace the present moment fully.

1. **Embracing Vulnerability:** Surrender requires a willingness to embrace vulnerability, acknowledging that we are not infallible and that life is inherently uncertain. It takes strength to acknowledge our limitations and relinquish the illusion of control.

   In doing so, we open ourselves to authentic connections and experiences, which can be transformative on both personal and professional levels.

2. **Trusting the Process:** Surrender involves placing trust in the inherent intelligence of life and the universe. Rather than trying to force outcomes, surrender invites us to trust that things will unfold as they are meant to, even if the path is unclear. It is a

testament to inner strength, as it demands patience, resilience, and the ability to maintain equanimity amid uncertainties.

3. **Releasing Attachment:** Surrendering necessitates detaching ourselves from specific outcomes or expectations. It is recognizing that our happiness and self-worth are not solely contingent on external achievements but are derived from within.

By letting go of attachment, we free ourselves from the constant anxiety and disappointment that arise when things don't go as planned.

4. **Cultivating Flexibility:** Surrender encourages a flexible and adaptive mindset. Rather than rigidly clinging to

fixed beliefs or plans, it urges us to be open to change and adjust our course when necessary. This adaptability is a mark of strength, as it allows us to navigate challenges with grace and resilience.

5. **Letting Go of Ego:** Surrendering involves transcending the ego's incessant need for validation and control. It is an act of humility that enables us to rise above the ego's limitations and discover a deeper sense of self.

   By releasing the ego's grip, we make room for growth, self-awareness, and spiritual evolution.

6. **Freedom from Stress:** Surrender liberates us from the burdensome weight of stress

and anxiety. When we stop fighting against the current of life and surrender to its natural flow, we experience a profound sense of peace and contentment. It is the strength to accept "what is" without resisting or dwelling on "what could have been."

7. **Empowerment through Choice:** Surrender is an active and conscious choice to let go rather than a passive acceptance of circumstances. It empowers us to focus our energy on things we can control, such as our attitude, actions, and responses to life's challenges.

By choosing surrender, we reclaim personal power and regain a sense of agency over our lives.

In conclusion, surrender is a dynamic and powerful concept that requires inner strength and courage. Far from implying weakness, surrender embodies the wisdom to release control, embrace vulnerability, and trust in the natural flow of life.

It is a profound act of self-awareness and liberation that opens the door to personal growth, resilience, and true fulfillment. When we learn to surrender with grace, we embark on a transformative journey of empowerment and inner peace.

BENEFITS OF SURRENDERING CONTROL

1. Reducing Stress and Anxiety: One of the most significant benefits of surrendering

control over things beyond our reach is a reduction in stress and anxiety.

When we accept that there are certain aspects of life beyond our control, we free ourselves from the constant worry and pressure to influence outcomes. This newfound freedom allows us to focus on the present moment and manage stress more effectively.

2. **Enhancing Emotional Well-being:** Surrendering control fosters emotional well-being by promoting acceptance and inner peace. When we stop struggling against circumstances we cannot change, we release ourselves from emotional turmoil.

This emotional liberation paves the way for increased contentment, joy, and resilience.

3. **Improving Relationships:** Surrendering control in relationships can lead to improved connections with others. Letting go of the need to control or change people allows us to appreciate them for who they are.

This acceptance creates a healthier and more harmonious dynamic, fostering deeper and more meaningful relationships.

4. **Increased Adaptability:** Surrendering control cultivates adaptability, a valuable trait in navigating life's challenges. By embracing the unpredictability of life, we

become better equipped to handle unexpected situations and changes.

This adaptability enables us to bounce back more swiftly from setbacks and view challenges as opportunities for growth.

5. **Fostering Patience:** Surrendering control requires patience, as we learn to wait and observe without intervening unnecessarily. This practice of patience helps us develop a more measured and thoughtful approach to decision-making and problem-solving.

6. **Resilience in the Face of Adversity:** Surrendering control strengthens our resilience. When faced with situations beyond our control, we become adept at accepting reality and finding constructive ways to move forward. This resilience is

essential in maintaining a positive outlook and persevering through difficult times.

7. **Freedom to Focus on What Matters:** Releasing control over uncontrollable aspects of life allows us to redirect our energy and focus toward what we can influence.

Instead of wasting time and effort on fruitless pursuits, we can channel our resources into meaningful endeavors, personal growth, and areas where we can make a difference.

8. **Improved Decision-Making:** Surrendering control fosters clarity in decision-making. When we accept that certain outcomes are beyond our grasp, we can focus on making choices based on

available information and personal values. This clarity leads to more confident and informed decisions.

9. **Enhancing Creativity and Innovation:** Surrendering control encourages a more open and curious mindset. When we let go of rigid expectations, we create space for creativity and innovative thinking.

This mindset shift allows us to explore new possibilities and approach challenges with fresh perspectives.

10. **Cultivating Gratitude:** Surrendering control can lead to a deeper sense of gratitude for the blessings in our lives. When we recognize that not everything is within our control, we become more

appreciative of the positive aspects and opportunities that come our way.

In conclusion, surrendering control over things beyond our reach is a powerful and transformative practice. It brings numerous benefits, including reduced stress, improved relationships, increased adaptability, and enhanced emotional well-being. By embracing surrender, we empower ourselves to navigate life's uncertainties with grace, resilience, and a greater sense of contentment.

PRACTICAL TIPS ON HOW TO EMBRACE SURRENDER AS A MEANS OF FINDING PEACE

Embracing surrender as a means of finding peace is a transformative practice that requires conscious effort and self-awareness. Here are some practical tips to help you incorporate surrender into your life and experience greater peace:

1. **Practice Mindfulness:** Mindfulness is the foundation of embracing surrender. Start by being present in the moment and observing your thoughts and emotions without judgment. This practice helps you become aware of any tendencies to resist or control situations.

2. **Identify Areas of Resistance:** Reflect on areas of your life where you struggle to let go of control. It could be related to work, relationships, health, or personal expectations. Recognizing these areas is the first step in actively working on surrendering.

3. **Cultivate Acceptance:** Embrace the idea that not everything in life is within your control. Practice accepting the things you cannot change, and focus your energy on what you can influence. Embracing acceptance allows you to find peace in the midst of uncertainty.

4. **Let Go of Expectations:** Release rigid expectations about how things should be and be open to different outcomes. Understand that life is full of surprises, and surrendering to the flow of events can lead to unexpected blessings and opportunities.

5. **Practice Detachment:** Detach yourself from the need to always be right or to have things go your way. Let go of the desire for approval and recognition from others. Detachment allows you to find

inner strength and peace independent of external circumstances.

6. **Trust in the Process:** Develop trust in the natural unfolding of life. Have faith that things will work out as they are meant to, even if the path is not clear at the moment. Trusting the process helps you let go of unnecessary worries and anxieties.

7. **Embrace Imperfection:** Surrendering involves accepting your imperfections and those of others. Embrace the idea that nobody is perfect, and mistakes are a natural part of growth and learning. Be compassionate toward yourself and others.

8. **Practice Letting Go Meditation:** Engage in meditation or visualization exercises that focus on letting go. Picture yourself releasing control and surrendering your

worries and fears. This practice can be deeply calming and grounding.

9. **Seek Support:** Share your journey of embracing surrender with friends, family, or a support group. Discussing your experiences and challenges with others can provide valuable insights and encouragement.

10. **Celebrate Progress:** Acknowledge and celebrate each step you take toward surrendering control. Finding peace through surrender is a gradual process, and it's essential to recognize your growth and efforts along the way.

Remember that embracing surrender is a continuous practice. Be patient with yourself and give yourself permission to experience moments of resistance without judgment. As you cultivate surrender, you'll discover a profound sense of peace and empowerment that comes from letting go and embracing the flow of life.

CHAPTER 2

RELEASING PAST HURTS

Introduction:

In the fast-paced world, the weight of past hurts can become an anchor, hindering personal growth and clouding our ability to thrive. Welcome to Chapter 2: "Releasing Past Hurts," where we embark on a transformative journey of healing and empowerment.

In this chapter, we delve into the profound impact of carrying emotional baggage from the past and explore the art of letting go. Just as a ship must jettison unnecessary cargo to sail smoothly, we too must release the burdens of past hurts to navigate our personal and professional lives with clarity and purpose.

Join us as we confront the ghosts of yesterday and uncover the keys to unshackling ourselves from the clutches of old wounds. Discover how releasing past hurts, liberates our hearts, renews our spirits, and opens the gateway to resilience and authentic success.

Prepare to be captivated by the liberating truths within these pages as we explore the immense power of letting go and the transformation that awaits on the horizon.

Are you ready to set sail towards a brighter, unburdened future? Let's embark on this captivating exploration together.

EMOTIONAL BAGGAGE HOLDING US BACK

Emotional baggage is the accumulation of unresolved emotions, traumas, and negative experiences from our past that continue to influence our present thoughts, behaviors, and beliefs. It can manifest as deep-seated fears, anger, resentment, guilt, or sadness. Here are some ways in which emotional baggage holds us back from living fully in the present:

1. **Negative Thought Patterns:** Emotional baggage often shapes our thought patterns, leading to negative self-talk and limiting beliefs. We may continuously replay past mistakes or painful experiences in our minds, creating a cycle of self-doubt and insecurity that hinders our present actions and decisions.

2. **Fear of Repeating Past Hurts:** Past traumas or heartaches can instill a fear of repeating those painful experiences in the present or future. This fear may cause us to avoid taking risks, stepping out of our comfort zones, and embracing new opportunities, limiting our personal and professional growth.

3. **Difficulty in Building Trust:** Unresolved emotional wounds can make it challenging to trust others fully. We may carry the fear of being hurt or betrayed again, which can lead to guarded and distant relationships, preventing us from forming meaningful connections.

4. **Inability to Let Go:** Holding onto emotional baggage can prevent us from forgiving ourselves or others for past mistakes. This inability to let go can lead

to a constant burden, making it hard to find peace and move forward.

5. **Diminished Emotional Well-being:** Carrying emotional baggage takes a toll on our emotional well-being. It can lead to heightened stress, anxiety, and even depression, making it difficult to find joy and contentment in the present moment.

6. **Lack of Presence and Mindfulness:** Dwelling on past hurts can distract us from being fully present in the here and now. We may miss out on the beauty and opportunities of the present moment, as our minds remain preoccupied with past experiences.

7. **Self-Sabotage:** Emotional baggage can unconsciously lead to self-sabotaging behaviors. We may undermine our own success and happiness because deep

down, we don't feel deserving or capable of achieving positive outcomes.

8. **Difficulty in Coping with Change:** Unresolved emotional baggage can make it harder to adapt to change. We may resist change out of fear of the unknown or because it triggers past unresolved emotions.

9. **Impact on Decision-making:** Our emotional baggage can cloud our judgment and influence our decision-making processes. We may make choices based on past wounds rather than on objective assessments of present situations.

10. **Strained Relationships:** The emotional baggage we carry can spill over into our relationships, causing conflicts,

misunderstandings, and barriers to effective communication.

In conclusion, emotional baggage has a profound impact on our ability to live fully in the present. It keeps us tied to the past, hindering personal growth, self-acceptance, and authentic living.

Recognizing and addressing our emotional baggage is a vital step toward finding peace, embracing the present, and creating a brighter future. By engaging in healing practices and letting go of the weight of the past, you will be free to fully experience the richness and opportunities that the present moment offers.

TECHNIQUES FOR LETTING GO OF PAST HURTS, GRUDGES, AND REGRETS

Letting go of past hurts, grudges, and regrets is a transformative process that requires time, self-compassion, and commitment to healing. Here are some techniques to help you release the emotional baggage and embrace a more positive and empowered outlook:

1. **Acknowledge and Validate Your Emotions:** Begin by acknowledging the pain and emotions associated with past hurts. Give yourself permission to feel whatever you're experiencing without judgment. Validate your emotions as a natural response to the experiences you've been through.

2. **Practice Forgiveness:** Forgiveness is a powerful tool for letting go of grudges and

regrets. This doesn't mean condoning or excusing the actions of others, but rather freeing yourself from the burden of carrying resentment. Forgive not for their sake but for your peace of mind.

3. **Write a Letter (Not Sent):** Consider writing a letter to the person who caused you pain or to yourself if the regret is self-directed. Pour out your feelings, express what you wish you could say, and allow yourself to process your emotions. This exercise can be cathartic and help you gain closure.

4. **Engage in Mindfulness and Meditation:** Mindfulness practices and meditation can help you become more aware of your thoughts and emotions without being overwhelmed by them. By staying present

and focused on the here and now, you can reduce rumination about the past.

5. **Practice Self-Compassion:** Be kind to yourself and avoid self-blame for past mistakes. Understand that everyone makes errors, and these experiences can be opportunities for growth and learning. Treat yourself with the same compassion you would offer a friend.

6. **Release Through Physical Activity:** Engage in physical activities that allow you to release pent-up emotions. Running, dancing, or engaging in yoga can help you process feelings and find relief.

7. **Seek Support:** Don't hesitate to seek support from friends, family, or a therapist. Talking about your feelings and experiences can provide validation and new perspectives to facilitate healing.

8. **Create a Ritual of Letting Go:** Consider creating a ritual that symbolizes your decision to let go of the past. This could involve writing down the hurts on paper and then burning or tearing the paper, symbolizing release and renewal.

9. **Focus on the Present and Future:** Shift your focus from dwelling on the past to embracing the present and looking forward to the future. Set new goals and create a vision for the life you want to lead, allowing positive aspirations to take center stage.

10. **Practice Gratitude:** Cultivate a daily gratitude practice to shift your attention to the positive aspects of your life. Focusing on what you're grateful for can help you reframe your perspective and reduce the

hold of past hurts on your present state of mind.

Remember that letting go is a process, and it's okay to take it one step at a time. Be patient with yourself and celebrate each small victory along the way. As you practice these techniques consistently, you will gradually experience a sense of liberation and empowerment as you release the weight of past hurts, grudges, and regrets.

LIBERATE YOUR HEART; THE HEALING POWER OF FORGIVENESS

The healing power of forgiveness is a profound force that can transform our emotional well-being and liberate our hearts from the chains of resentment and pain. When we choose to forgive, we free ourselves from the burden of carrying past hurts and open the door to emotional healing and inner peace. Here's how forgiveness works its transformative magic:

1. **Releasing Emotional Baggage:** Forgiveness is like a cleansing balm for the heart. By forgiving others or even ourselves, we release the emotional baggage we have been carrying. This release lifts the weight from our hearts, allowing us to breathe freely and unburdening ourselves from the pain of the past.

2. **Healing Emotional Wounds:** Unresolved emotional wounds can fester and affect various aspects of our lives. When we forgive, we acknowledge our pain, confront it, and take steps to heal. This

healing process can be both cathartic and transformative, leading to emotional growth and resilience.

3. **Empowering Self-Liberation:** Forgiveness is an act of self-liberation. It is not about condoning or excusing the actions of others, but about breaking free from the control they have had over our emotions. When we forgive, we take back our power and regain control over how we feel.

4. **Restoring Inner Peace:** Holding onto grudges and anger can leave us in a perpetual state of turmoil. Forgiveness, on the other hand, restores inner peace. It creates a sense of calmness and tranquility within ourselves, enabling us to focus on positivity and growth.

5. **Breaking Cycles of Pain:** By forgiving, we break the cycles of pain and hurt that may have been perpetuating for generations. We have the power to stop the spread of negativity and transform it into compassion and understanding.

6. **Deepening Empathy and Compassion:** Forgiveness deepens our capacity for empathy and compassion. As we recognize the imperfections and vulnerabilities of others, we become more understanding and accepting of human fallibility.

7. **Enhancing Relationships:** In relationships, forgiveness can be a powerful healing tool. It allows us to repair damaged connections and rebuild trust. It fosters an environment of

understanding and empathy, strengthening the bond between individuals.

8. **Fostering Emotional Resilience:** Forgiving others and ourselves contributes to emotional resilience. It equips us to face challenges with grace and a greater sense of self-awareness. Resilience enables us to bounce back from adversities and maintain emotional balance.

9. **Promoting Positive Mental Health:** The act of forgiveness positively impacts mental health. It reduces stress, anxiety, and depression, promoting a healthier emotional state and a more positive outlook on life.

10. **Opening the Door to Love and Joy:** Forgiveness clears the path for love and joy to flourish. As we liberate our hearts

from negativity, we create space for love and joy to enter and enrich our lives.

In conclusion, forgiveness is a transformative and liberating force. It is an act of compassion and self-empowerment that enables us to heal emotional wounds, release past hurts, and find inner peace. By embracing forgiveness, we unlock the healing power within our hearts, setting ourselves on a path toward emotional freedom and a more fulfilling life.

CHAPTER 3

BREAKING FREE FROM FEAR AND ANXIETY

INTRODUCTION

In the fast-paced world, fear and anxiety acts as relentless roadblocks, hindering growth and stifling potential. Welcome to Chapter 3: "Breaking Free from Fear and Anxiety," where we embark on a powerful journey to liberate ourselves from the chains of self-doubt and hesitation.

In this chapter, we confront the fears that hold us back and explore strategies to overcome anxiety in the pursuit of success and fulfillment. Just as a bird needs to break free from its cage to soar, we too must liberate ourselves from the limitations of fear and anxiety to unleash our true potential.

Join us as we delve into the psychology of fear, dissecting its impact on decision-making and performance. Together, we'll discover how to cultivate resilience, embrace uncertainty, and develop a mindset of courage to thrive in the face of challenges.

Prepare to be captivated by the empowering truths within these pages as we unveil the tools to navigate fear and anxiety. It's time to break free from the shackles of fear and step into a world of boundless opportunities and achievements.

Are you **ready** to **conquer fear** and **anxiety** and unlock your **full** potential? Let's embark on this captivating exploration together.

THE FEARS AND ANXIETIES THAT LIMIT OUR POTENTIAL AND HAPPINESS

1. **Fear of Failure:** The fear of failure is a common barrier that holds many people back from pursuing their goals. It creates self-doubt, diminishes confidence, and prevents individuals from taking risks or stepping out of their comfort zones.

   Overcoming this fear involves reframing failure as a stepping stone to growth and learning, rather than a sign of inadequacy.

2. **Fear of Rejection:** The fear of rejection can hinder social interactions and networking opportunities. It may lead to avoidance of new relationships or reluctance to express opinions and ideas.

Addressing this fear requires building self-esteem and understanding that rejection is a part of life, and it doesn't define one's worth.

3. **Fear of Uncertainty:** The fear of uncertainty can paralyze decision-making and hinder progress. Accepting that uncertainty is an inherent part of life helps to build resilience and adaptability. Focusing on what can be controlled and embracing ambiguity can ease anxiety surrounding the unknown.

4. **Fear of Public Speaking:** Public speaking anxiety can impede career advancement and networking opportunities. Addressing this fear involves practicing public speaking, seeking support from mentors or coaches,

and realizing that nervousness is normal and manageable.

5. **Fear of Success:** The fear of success may seem counterintuitive, but it can stem from the pressure to maintain achievements or fear of the changes that come with success. Exploring the underlying beliefs and expectations surrounding success is crucial to overcoming this fear.

6. **Anxiety about Work-Life Balance:** Balancing work and personal life can be a source of anxiety. Setting boundaries, prioritizing self-care, and establishing clear communication with employers or colleagues can alleviate this anxiety.

7. **Fear of Change:** The fear of change can hinder personal and professional growth. Embracing change as an opportunity for

growth and viewing it as a chance to learn and adapt can help overcome this fear.

8. **Anxiety about the Future:** Worrying excessively about the future can rob individuals of their present joy and productivity. Practicing mindfulness and focusing on the present moment can reduce anxiety about the future.

9. **Fear of Criticism and Judgment:** The fear of criticism and judgment can stifle creativity and self-expression. Learning to detach self-worth from external validation and seeking constructive feedback can help manage this fear.

10. **Anxiety about Financial Security:** Worries about financial stability can create stress and anxiety. Creating a financial plan, budgeting, and seeking professional advice can alleviate these concerns.

In conclusion, addressing the fears and anxieties that limit our potential and happiness is a journey of self-awareness and personal growth. By understanding the roots of these fears and adopting strategies to cope with them, we can break free from their grip and unlock our true potential for success and happiness. Embracing courage, resilience, and a positive mindset can pave the way to a more fulfilling and enriching life.

STRATEGIES FOR CONFRONTING AND RELEASING FEARS

1. **Identify and Acknowledge Fears:** Start by identifying the specific fears that are holding you back. Acknowledge them without judgment, and recognize that it is normal to have fears and anxieties.

Awareness is the first step toward addressing them.

2. **Challenge Negative Beliefs:** Examine the beliefs that underlie your fears. Challenge any negative and limiting beliefs that may not be based on reality. Replace them with more positive and empowering beliefs that support your growth and potential.

3. **Set Realistic Goals:** Break down your larger goals into smaller, achievable steps. This helps to reduce the overwhelming nature of fear, as you can focus on taking one step at a time.

4. **Visualize Success:** Use visualization techniques to imagine yourself successfully confronting your fears and achieving your goals. Visualization can create a sense of confidence and

familiarity, making the actual experience less intimidating.

5. **Practice Mindfulness:** Cultivate mindfulness to stay present and aware of your thoughts and emotions. Mindfulness can help you recognize fear-based thought patterns and prevent them from spiraling out of control.

6. **Seek Support:** Reach out to friends, family, or a mentor for support and encouragement. Talking about your fears can provide valuable insights and different perspectives, helping you confront and release them.

7. **Exposure Therapy:** Gradually expose yourself to the situations that trigger fear or anxiety. Start with small steps and gradually increase exposure. Over time,

this can desensitize you to the fear and build confidence.

8. **Seek Professional Help:** If fears and anxieties significantly impact your daily life or hinder your progress, consider seeking help from a therapist or counselor. They can provide tools and techniques tailored to your specific needs.

9. **Practice Self-Compassion:** Be kind to yourself as you confront your fears. Understand that it's okay to feel afraid and that it takes time and effort to release deeply ingrained fears. Treat yourself with the same compassion you would offer to a friend.

10. **Celebrate Progress:** Acknowledge and celebrate each step you take in confronting and releasing your fears. Celebrating progress reinforces positive

behavior and builds motivation to continue moving forward.

11. **Use Positive Affirmations:** Repeat positive affirmations daily to reinforce a positive mindset and counteract fear-based thoughts. Affirmations can help shift your focus to more empowering beliefs.

12. **Embrace a Growth Mindset:** Embrace the idea that failure is a part of growth and learning. Emphasize the process rather than fixating on outcomes, and view challenges as opportunities for self-improvement.

Remember that confronting and releasing fears is a gradual process, and it's okay to take small steps. Be patient with yourself and practice these strategies consistently. With time and dedication, you can break free from the limitations of fear and embrace a more empowered and fulfilling life.

THE TRANSFORMATIVE POWER OF FACING FEARS AND EMBRACING UNCERTAINTY

Embracing uncertainty and facing our fears have the transformative power to unlock hidden potentials, catalyze personal growth, and lead us to a more fulfilling and resilient life. Here's how confronting fears and embracing uncertainty can be truly transformative:

1. **Building Resilience:** When we face our fears and embrace uncertainty, we develop resilience—the ability to bounce back from challenges and setbacks. Each time we confront a fear, we become stronger

and more adept at navigating life's uncertainties.

2. **Expanding Comfort Zones:** Embracing uncertainty involves stepping outside of our comfort zones. As we venture into the unknown, our comfort zones expand, allowing us to take on new opportunities and experiences with greater confidence.

3. **Discovering Hidden Strengths:** Facing fears often reveals inner strengths and capabilities we never knew we possessed. We tap into courage, determination, and perseverance that lie dormant until we confront our fears head-on.

4. **Enhancing Self-Confidence:** Each time we successfully confront a fear, our self-confidence grows. Embracing uncertainty and stepping into the unknown helps us recognize our own abilities and

potential, fostering a deep sense of self-assurance.

5. **Cultivating Adaptability:** Embracing uncertainty requires us to adapt to changing circumstances. This adaptability becomes a valuable skill in navigating life's twists and turns, making us more flexible and better equipped to handle challenges.

6. **Opening Doors to New Opportunities:** Confronting fears and embracing uncertainty often leads us to new opportunities and experiences we might have otherwise missed. It broadens our horizons and exposes us to paths we never thought possible.

7. **Empowering Decision-Making:** When we face our fears, we gain a clearer perspective on what truly matters to us.

This clarity empowers us to make decisions aligned with our values and aspirations, rather than being driven by fear or avoidance.

8. **Overcoming Limiting Beliefs:** Confronting fears challenges the limiting beliefs that hold us back. Embracing uncertainty helps us question and discard these self-imposed limitations, allowing us to reach new heights of achievement.

9. **Fostering Innovation and Creativity:** Embracing uncertainty encourages us to think outside the box and explore new possibilities. It sparks creativity and innovation, as we seek alternative solutions to the challenges that arise.

10. **Embracing the Journey:** Confronting fears and embracing uncertainty shifts our focus from fixating on outcomes to

embracing the journey itself. We learn to find joy and fulfillment in the process of growth and self-discovery.

11. **Living Authentically:** Facing fears enables us to live authentically and in alignment with our true selves. As we shed the layers of fear, we become more authentic in our relationships and pursuits.

12. **Creating a Life of Fulfillment:** Ultimately, confronting fears and embracing uncertainty leads us to a life of greater fulfillment. We become more attuned to our passions and purpose, shaping a life that is meaningful and enriching.

In conclusion, the transformative power of facing fears and embracing uncertainty is profound. It liberates us from self-imposed limitations, opens doors to new possibilities, and empowers us to lead lives of resilience, authenticity, and fulfillment. By embracing the unknown with courage and curiosity, we unlock the true potential within ourselves and embark on a journey of growth and self-discovery that transcends our wildest imaginations.

CHAPTER 4

DETACHING FROM OUTCOMES

Introduction

In this dynamic world, the desire for specific outcomes can become a double-edged sword—propelling us forward but also clouding our judgment. Welcome to CHAPTER 4: "Detaching from Outcomes," where we explore the transformative power of relinquishing the need for rigid results.

In this chapter, we confront the pitfalls of outcome fixation and delve into the liberating art of letting go. Just as a skilled archer releases the arrow without fixating on the target, we too must learn to detach from outcomes to find true clarity and focus.

Join us as we navigate the delicate balance between ambition and equanimity, discovering how releasing attachment to results unleashes our creativity, enhances decision-making, and cultivates a resilient and adaptable mindset.

Prepare to be captivated by the empowering wisdom within these pages as we embrace the art of surrendering control over outcomes, empowering us to thrive in the ever-changing tides of this world.

Are you ready to release the burden of outcomes and unlock the potential of present-moment excellence? Let's embark on this captivating exploration together.

TENDENCY TO ATTACH OUR HAPPINESS TO SPECIFIC OUTCOMES AND HOW IT CAN LEAD TO DISAPPOINTMENT.

The tendency to attach our happiness to specific outcomes is a common human trait, and it can have significant consequences on our emotional well-being and overall life satisfaction. When we tie our happiness solely to achieving particular goals or obtaining specific results, we set ourselves up for potential disappointment in the following ways:

1. **Conditional Happiness:** Attaching happiness to specific outcomes creates conditional happiness. We condition our joy and contentment on achieving those outcomes, making it contingent on external factors beyond our control. This

leaves us vulnerable to fluctuations in circumstances and undermines our ability to find happiness in the present moment.

2. **Limited Perspective:** Outcome-based happiness narrows our perspective and focus. We become fixated on the end result, disregarding the journey, growth, and learning opportunities along the way.

This limited perspective may lead to neglecting the value of the process and the smaller victories achieved during the pursuit of our goals.

3. **Vulnerability to Disappointment:** When our happiness is tied to specific outcomes, any deviation from the expected results can lead to disappointment and a sense of failure. This disappointment can be deeply

disheartening, especially if we invest significant time and effort into pursuing those outcomes.

4. **Reduced Resilience:** The link between happiness and specific outcomes can reduce our resilience in the face of setbacks. Failure to achieve desired results may lead to self-doubt, demotivation, and a reluctance to try again, hindering our ability to bounce back from adversity.

5. **Fear of Failure:** When happiness hinges on specific outcomes, the fear of failure intensifies. This fear can lead to avoidance of taking risks or trying new things, as we fear the potential negative impact on our happiness if we don't succeed.

6. **Comparison and Envy:** Tying happiness to outcomes can lead to unhealthy comparison with others who have

achieved similar goals. Envy may arise if others appear more successful, creating feelings of inadequacy and discontentment.

7. **Lack of Contentment:** If we continually chase specific outcomes to find happiness, we may never feel truly content. The constant pursuit of more can lead to a perpetual feeling of dissatisfaction, as there will always be new goals to achieve.

8. **Overlooking the Present:** Outcome-based happiness can cause us to overlook the present moment. We may become preoccupied with future achievements, missing out on the beauty and opportunities available in the here and now.

9. **Neglecting Personal Growth:** Focusing solely on outcomes may lead us to neglect

the importance of personal growth and self-development. The journey of growth is as crucial as the destination, and attaching happiness to outcomes may hinder our willingness to explore and evolve.

10. Interference with Relationships: The pressure of achieving specific outcomes can interfere with relationships. We may become so driven by our goals that we neglect the needs and experiences of those around us.

In conclusion, attaching our happiness to specific outcomes can lead to disappointment and hinder our overall well-being. It limits our perspective, reduces resilience, and perpetuates conditional happiness. Liberating ourselves from this attachment allows us to find joy in the journey, appreciate the present, and cultivate a more resilient and contented approach to life.

Embracing a mindset that values the process of growth and acknowledges the worth of every step, regardless of the outcome, can lead to greater fulfillment and inner peace.

STAY MOTIVATED AND PROACTIVE BY DETACHING FROM OUTCOMES

Detaching from outcomes while staying motivated and proactive is a delicate balance that requires mindfulness and a shift in mindset. Here are some strategies to help you achieve this balance:

1. **Focus on Process Goals:** Instead of fixating solely on the end result, set process-oriented goals. Focus on the

actions and steps you need to take to reach your desired outcomes. Celebrate the progress you make along the way, irrespective of the final outcome.

2. **Clarify Your Values:** Understand your values and align your goals with them. When your goals are rooted in your core values, the process becomes more meaningful, regardless of the outcome. This connection enhances motivation and fulfillment.

3. **Embrace a Growth Mindset:** Adopt a growth mindset that sees challenges and setbacks as opportunities for learning and improvement. Embrace the idea that progress and development are more important than achieving a particular outcome.

4. **Practice Mindfulness:** Cultivate mindfulness to stay present and aware of your thoughts and emotions. Mindfulness helps you detach from excessive worry about the future and enhances your ability to stay focused on the present moment.

5. **Set Realistic Expectations:** Be realistic about the outcomes you can achieve and the time it may take to reach your goals. Unrealistic expectations can lead to disappointment and frustration.

6. **Visualize the Process, Not Just the Outcome:** Visualization can be a powerful tool, but instead of focusing solely on the end result, visualize yourself engaged in the process of working towards your goals. See yourself taking the necessary steps and enjoying the journey.

7. **Celebrate Effort and Progress:** Acknowledge and celebrate the effort and progress you make, regardless of whether you achieve your desired outcomes. Rewarding yourself for your hard work can reinforce a proactive and motivated approach.

8. **Practice Gratitude:** Cultivate gratitude for the opportunities and resources you have to pursue your goals. Gratitude shifts your focus from what you lack to what you have, fostering a positive and proactive mindset.

9. **Maintain a Growth-Oriented Support System:** Surround yourself with people who support your growth and share a similar outlook. Seek encouragement from friends, mentors, or colleagues who appreciate the process of progress.

10. **Learn from Setbacks:** When setbacks occur, view them as learning experiences rather than failures. Analyze what you can learn from the situation and use that knowledge to adapt your approach moving forward.

11. **Stay Adaptable:** Embrace the idea that outcomes may change, and new opportunities may arise. Staying adaptable allows you to adjust your goals and strategies when necessary, keeping you proactive in the face of uncertainty.

12. **Practice Self-Compassion:** Be kind to yourself when things don't go as planned. Avoid self-criticism and practice self-compassion, understanding that detaching from outcomes is a process that takes time and practice.

By incorporating these strategies into your daily life, you can detach from outcomes while maintaining motivation and proactivity. Remember that the journey towards detaching from outcomes is ongoing, and be patient with yourself as you cultivate this empowering and growth-oriented mindset.

THE FREEDOM GAINED FROM NOT BEING OVERLY ATTACHED TO RESULTS

Imagine a skilled tightrope walker stepping onto a narrow rope, suspended high above the ground. As they start walking, their focus remains on each step, feeling the balance, and adjusting accordingly. The audience watches in awe, witnessing a breathtaking display of grace and control.

What makes this performance so extraordinary is not just the successful completion of the tightrope walk but the profound freedom the tightrope walker experiences by not being overly attached to the end result.

In life, just like the tightrope walker, when we detach from being overly attached to results, we gain an unparalleled sense of freedom:

1. **Embracing the Present Moment:** Without the heavy burden of outcome-driven pressure, we immerse ourselves fully in the present moment. We can focus on the task at hand, savoring the experience, and appreciating the journey.

2. **Fearlessness in Taking Risks:** Detaching from results empowers us to take bold risks. We become unafraid of failure,

knowing that it does not define us but rather offers lessons for growth and improvement.

3. **Creative Exploration:** With the weight of expectations lifted, our creativity flourishes. We are free to explore new possibilities, innovate, and think outside the box.

4. **Resilience in the Face of Setbacks:** When results do not meet our expectations, we bounce back with resilience. The lack of attachment allows us to reevaluate, adjust, and continue moving forward with renewed determination.

5. **Freedom to Pursue Passion:** Detachment liberates us to pursue our passions without the fear of judgment or failure. We can

wholeheartedly invest ourselves in what brings us joy and fulfillment.

6. **Cultivating Inner Peace:** The absence of outcome-driven stress brings inner peace. We release the constant anxiety about the future and find tranquility in the present moment.

7. **Improved Decision-Making:** Not being fixated on specific results enables clearer and more objective decision-making. We can focus on what aligns with our values and long-term vision rather than short-term gains.

8. **Strengthened Relationships:** Detachment enhances our relationships, as we are more present and authentic in our interactions. We connect with others genuinely, rather than being driven by ulterior motives.

9. **Personal Growth and Learning:** By detaching from results, we become open to growth and learning. We embrace new challenges, knowing that every experience contributes to our development.

10. **Reduced Stress and Anxiety:** The freedom from excessive attachment to outcomes leads to reduced stress and anxiety. We let go of the need for external validation and find peace in our self-worth.

11. **Appreciating Small Victories:** Without the fixation on monumental achievements, we celebrate the small victories and milestones along the way. Each step becomes a triumph in itself.

12. **Living Authentically:** Detachment allows us to live authentically, true to ourselves and our values. We are not

swayed by external pressures but guided by our inner compass.

In conclusion, detaching from being overly attached to results bestows a profound freedom that transcends conventional notions of success. Like the tightrope walker, we learn to navigate the challenges of life gracefully, focusing on the present and embracing each step without being consumed by the destination. This freedom empowers us to live with passion, resilience, and authenticity, unlocking the full potential of a life truly well-lived.

CHAPTER 5

LETTING GO OF CONTROL IN RELATIONSHIPS

Introduction:

Welcome to Chapter 5: "Letting Go of Control in Relationships," where we explore the transformative power of relinquishing the need to micromanage and dictate outcomes in our professional and personal connections.

In this chapter, we confront the detrimental effects of excessive control on relationships and delve into the liberating art of trust and empowerment. Just as a skilled conductor allows the orchestra to thrive independently, we too must learn to embrace the harmony that comes from letting go of the reins.

Join us as we navigate the delicate balance between leadership and collaboration, discovering how releasing the grip on control fosters open communication, strengthens bonds, and fosters a culture of autonomy and innovation.

Prepare to be captivated by the empowering insights within these pages as we embrace the art of empowering relationships, cultivating a dynamic landscape of cooperation and growth.

Are you ready to unleash the potential of authentic connections and create a thriving network of trust and collaboration? Let's embark on this captivating exploration together.

THE CHALLENGES OF CONTROL IN RELATIONSHIPS AND HOW IT AFFECTS OUR CONNECTIONS WITH OTHERS.

Control in relationships can present numerous challenges and have a significant impact on our connections with others. Let's examine some of the key challenges of control and its effects on relationships:

1. **Erosion of Trust:** Excessive control erodes trust between individuals. When one person consistently seeks to dominate or manipulate the other, it creates an environment of suspicion and skepticism. Trust is the foundation of healthy relationships, and control undermines this crucial element.

2. **Communication Breakdown:** Control often leads to poor communication. The

person exerting control may not listen to others' perspectives or dismiss their input, stifling open dialogue and hindering the sharing of ideas.

3. **Resentment and Rebellion:** Being subjected to control can breed feelings of resentment and rebellion in the other person. They may feel suffocated or undervalued, leading to passive-aggressive behavior or outright resistance.

4. **Lack of Autonomy:** Control diminishes individual autonomy and empowerment. People may feel like they have no say in decisions that affect them, leading to a loss of motivation and engagement.

5. **Impact on Emotional Well-Being:** Being under the constant scrutiny and control of another person can lead to increased

stress, anxiety, and a sense of powerlessness. This negative impact on emotional well-being can spill over into other aspects of life.

6. **Inhibition of Growth:** Control stifles personal and professional growth. People may avoid taking risks or exploring new opportunities, fearing disapproval or punishment.

7. **Deterioration of Intimacy:** Intimacy requires vulnerability and trust. Control erects barriers that prevent authentic emotional connections, leading to emotional distance and isolation.

8. **Imbalance of Power:** Control often creates an imbalance of power in relationships, with one person assuming a dominant role. This imbalance can lead to an unhealthy dynamic where the

controlled person feels powerless and undervalued.

9. **Impact on Team Dynamics:** In professional settings, control within teams can disrupt collaboration and diminish creativity. When team members feel micromanaged, they may become reluctant to share ideas or take ownership of their work.

10. **Resistance to Feedback:** Those exerting control may be resistant to feedback or alternative viewpoints. This can hinder growth and prevent the recognition of opportunities for improvement.

11. **Interference with Decision-Making:** Control can hinder effective decision-making processes. When one person insists on imposing their ideas

without considering others' input, it can lead to suboptimal outcomes.

12. Strain on Relationships: Ultimately, control puts a strain on relationships, leading to dissatisfaction and potential conflicts. It can damage the fabric of connections, making it challenging to rebuild trust and repair the damage done.

In conclusion, the challenges of control in relationships are far-reaching and deeply impactful. It hampers communication, erodes trust, and inhibits growth and intimacy.

Striking a balance between asserting leadership and empowering others is essential to foster healthy, collaborative connections that thrive on trust, respect, and mutual support. By recognizing and addressing the challenges of control, we can create a nurturing environment that encourages the growth and flourishing of both individuals and relationships.

GUIDANCE ON HOW TO FOSTER TRUST AND OPEN COMMUNICATION

Fostering trust and open communication is essential for building strong and healthy relationships, whether in personal or professional settings. Here are some valuable guidance to achieve this:

1. **Active Listening:** Practice active listening, giving your full attention to the other person without interrupting or formulating responses in your mind. Show empathy and understanding, validating their feelings and perspectives.

2. **Be Transparent:** Be open and honest in your communication. Avoid hiding information or withholding important details, as this can erode trust over time.

3. **Keep Commitments:** Honor your commitments and follow through on your promises. Reliability and consistency build trust and credibility in relationships.

4. **Share Vulnerabilities:** Being vulnerable and sharing your thoughts and feelings creates an atmosphere of trust. It encourages others to reciprocate, fostering deeper connections.

5. **Avoid Blame and Judgment:** Focus on problem-solving instead of placing blame or passing judgment. Create a safe space where people feel comfortable expressing their ideas and concerns.

6. **Respect Boundaries:** Respect others' boundaries and personal space. Avoid prying into sensitive matters, and be mindful of their comfort levels during conversations.

7. **Encourage Feedback:** Invite feedback and constructive criticism from others. Appreciate and learn from their insights, as this demonstrates that you value their input.

8. **Be Non-Defensive:** When receiving feedback or criticism, remain open and non-defensive. Acknowledge your mistakes and show a willingness to improve.

9. **Clarify Misunderstandings:** Misunderstandings can lead to distrust. If there is a miscommunication, address it

promptly and clarify any confusion to avoid further complications.

10. **Celebrate Successes Together:** Acknowledge and celebrate individual and collective achievements. Recognizing accomplishments fosters a sense of teamwork and camaraderie.

11. **Resolve Conflicts Constructively:** Conflict is natural in relationships, but approach it with a constructive mindset. Seek resolutions that address the issue at hand while preserving the relationship.

12. **Value Different Perspectives:** Embrace diversity of thought and encourage different perspectives. This enriches discussions and leads to innovative solutions.

13. **Give and Receive Feedback Gracefully:** When providing feedback, be

constructive and considerate of the other person's feelings. When receiving feedback, be receptive and show appreciation for the input.

14. **Build Emotional Intelligence:** Develop emotional intelligence to understand and manage your emotions effectively. This skill helps navigate challenging conversations with empathy and self-awareness.

15. **Be Patient:** Building trust and open communication takes time. Be patient and persistent in nurturing these qualities within your relationships.

By incorporating these guiding principles into your interactions, you create an environment of trust and open communication. This foundation supports strong, collaborative relationships that foster growth, innovation, and meaningful connections with others.

THE BEAUTY OF ALLOWING OTHERS TO BE THEMSELVES WITHOUT TRYING TO CHANGE THEM.

Allowing others to be themselves without trying to change them is a truly beautiful and transformative aspect of relationships. Here's why it is so valuable:

1. **Authenticity:** When we let others be themselves, we encourage authenticity. People feel free to express their true thoughts, feelings, and personalities without fear of judgment or rejection. This fosters genuine connections based on honesty and openness.

2. **Respect and Acceptance:** Allowing others to be themselves demonstrates respect and acceptance. It shows that we value and appreciate them for who they are, not for who we want them to be. This acceptance builds a foundation of trust and comfort in the relationship.

3. **Nurturing Growth:** When people are allowed to be themselves, they can explore their interests, passions, and strengths fully. This exploration leads to personal growth and self-discovery, enriching their lives and relationships.

4. **Emotional Safety:** Creating an environment where people can be themselves promotes emotional safety. They feel secure to share their vulnerabilities, knowing they won't be judged or criticized.

5. **Enhanced Communication:** When individuals are free to be themselves, communication becomes more authentic and open. This transparency fosters deeper understanding and connection between people.

6. **Positive Energy:** Allowing others to be themselves brings a positive energy to the relationship. It encourages a sense of ease and comfort, making interactions enjoyable and uplifting.

7. **Appreciation of Differences:** Embracing others as they are highlights the beauty of diversity. We learn to appreciate and celebrate the differences that make each individual unique.

8. **Unconditional Love:** Allowing others to be themselves demonstrates unconditional love and support. It conveys the message

that we care for them without any expectations or conditions.

9. **Strengthening Relationships:** Embracing others as they are strengthens the bond in relationships. It creates a space where people feel cherished, fostering deeper emotional connections.

10. **Inspiration and Creativity:** When individuals are encouraged to be themselves, they are more likely to share their ideas and creativity openly. This exchange of ideas leads to mutual inspiration and innovation.

11. **Freedom from Judgment:** By not trying to change others, we free ourselves from the burden of judgment. We accept people as they are, embracing their imperfections and quirks with love and understanding.

12. Harmony and Balance: Allowing others to be themselves creates a harmonious and balanced relationship dynamic. It promotes a sense of ease and flow, where each person's uniqueness is honored and appreciated.

In conclusion, allowing others to be themselves without trying to change them is a beautiful gift we can give to ourselves and those we cherish. It fosters authenticity, respect, and acceptance, creating a safe and nurturing space for personal growth and genuine connections. Embracing and celebrating the individuality of others enriches our lives, leading to more fulfilling and meaningful relationships.

CHAPTER 6

EMBRACING CHANGE AND IMPERMANENCE

Introduction:

Welcome to Chapter 6: "Embracing Change and Impermanence," where we explore the art of gracefully navigating the ever-evolving landscape of life.

In this chapter, we confront the inevitability of change and the impermanence of all things, unveiling the transformative power of embracing uncertainty. Just as a skilled sailor adjusts the sails to catch changing winds, we too must learn to thrive amidst the ebb and flow of an ever-shifting world.

Join us as we navigate the uncharted waters of adaptability and resilience, discovering how embracing change ignites innovation, fosters growth, and propels us to new heights of success.

Prepare to be captivated by the empowering insights within these pages as we embrace the fluidity of change, cultivating a mindset that turns challenges into opportunities and uncertainty into our greatest ally.

Are you ready to chart a course that harnesses the winds of change to lead you to uncharted territories of greatness? Let's embark on this captivating exploration together.

THE INEVITABILITY OF CHANGE AND IMPERMANENCE IN LIFE.

The inevitability of change and impermanence is a fundamental aspect of life that touches every living being and entity. From the smallest organisms to the grandest galaxies, everything in the universe is subject to constant transformation. Understanding and accepting this reality is crucial for navigating life with resilience, wisdom, and a sense of wonder. Let's discuss comprehensively about the inevitability of change and impermanence in life:

1. **Nature's Cycles:** In nature, the cycles of birth, growth, decay, and rebirth are evident everywhere. Seasons change, tides ebb and flow, and plants bloom and wither. These cyclical patterns remind us

that change is a natural and essential part of life.

2. **Personal Growth and Development:** As individuals, we experience change from the moment we are born. Physically, emotionally, and intellectually, we continuously evolve and develop throughout our lives. Each stage of life brings unique experiences and challenges, contributing to our personal growth.

3. **Social and Cultural Evolution:** Societies and cultures also undergo transformation over time. Traditions, beliefs, and norms evolve, reflecting the changing needs and aspirations of communities. Embracing these changes allows societies to progress and adapt.

4. **Career and Professional Life:** In the professional realm, industries,

technologies, and job markets are in a constant state of flux. Being open to learning, re-skilling, and adapting to change is essential for career growth and success.

5. **Relationships:** Relationships, too, are subject to change. People come into our lives, and some may depart. The dynamics of friendships, romantic partnerships, and family ties evolve over time, calling for flexibility and understanding.

6. **Health and Aging:** Our physical health and vitality also experience changes with age. Accepting the impermanence of our youth and embracing the wisdom and experiences that come with aging can lead to a more fulfilling life journey.

7. **Global Events and Circumstances:** Global events, such as economic shifts,

political changes, and natural disasters, impact societies and individuals. Adapting to these external forces requires resilience and a willingness to embrace change.

8. **Learning from Impermanence:** The impermanence of life teaches us valuable lessons. It reminds us to cherish moments of joy, seek growth in times of adversity, and let go of attachments that no longer serve us.

9. **Coping with Loss and Grief:** Understanding impermanence helps us cope with loss and grief. Recognizing that everything has its season can offer solace during challenging times.

10. **Finding Freedom:** Embracing change and impermanence can free us from the burden of clinging to fixed expectations. It

opens us to new possibilities and liberates us from the fear of the unknown.

11. **Embracing the Present Moment:** Embracing impermanence encourages us to live in the present moment. By savoring the here and now, we find deeper joy and appreciation for the beauty of life's fleeting moments.

12. **Spiritual Insights:** Many spiritual traditions teach the impermanence of all things as a core tenet. Accepting impermanence can lead to profound spiritual insights, fostering a deeper connection with ourselves and the universe.

In conclusion, the inevitability of change and impermanence is an undeniable truth of life. By acknowledging and embracing this reality, we can cultivate a more profound sense of acceptance, resilience, and gratitude.

Embracing change allows us to grow, innovate, and adapt, while acknowledging impermanence invites us to cherish and make the most of the precious moments we have. Life's impermanence is what makes it a beautiful and awe-inspiring journey, filled with opportunities for growth, wisdom, and connection with the ever-changing world around us.

EMBRACING CHANGE CAN LEAD TO GROWTH AND NEW OPPORTUNITIES.

Embracing change leads to growth and new opportunities in various aspects of life. Let's explore comprehensively how this process unfolds:

1. Adaptability and Resilience: Embracing change cultivates adaptability and resilience. When faced with new situations, we learn to adjust our mindset, skills, and strategies, making us more adept at handling future challenges.

2. Learning and Development: Change often presents us with opportunities to learn and acquire new knowledge. Whether it's acquiring new skills for a changing job market or adapting to technological advancements, embracing change fuels continuous learning and personal development.

3. **Innovation and Creativity:** Change prompts us to think differently and approach problems with fresh perspectives. Embracing change fosters creativity and innovation, leading to the

development of new ideas, products, and solutions.

4. **Discovering Strengths:** During times of change, we may uncover untapped strengths and capabilities within ourselves. Overcoming challenges and stepping out of our comfort zones can reveal hidden potentials.

5. **Stepping Out of Comfort Zones:** Embracing change pushes us to step out of our comfort zones. By doing so, we expand our horizons and embrace opportunities that were previously overlooked or feared.

6. **Breaking Limiting Beliefs:** Change challenges our limiting beliefs and assumptions. Embracing change enables us to question these self-imposed limitations and discover our true potential.

7. **Building Confidence:** Successfully navigating change builds confidence. As we adapt and overcome obstacles, we gain the assurance that we can handle future uncertainties with grace and courage.

8. **Networking and Collaboration:** Embracing change often involves connecting with new people and forming collaborations. New opportunities arise as we expand our network and collaborate with diverse perspectives and talents.

9. **Career Growth:** Embracing change in the workplace can lead to career advancement. Demonstrating adaptability and a willingness to take on new challenges can catch the attention of employers and open doors for growth.

10. **Evolving Goals and Priorities:** Change can lead to reevaluating our goals and

priorities. Embracing change empowers us to align our aspirations with our evolving values and life circumstances.

11. **Overcoming Fear of Failure:** Embracing change helps us confront the fear of failure. As we accept that change is inevitable and failure is a natural part of growth, we become more willing to take calculated risks.

12. **Seeing Opportunities in Setbacks:** Change can sometimes bring setbacks, but embracing it enables us to see opportunities in those setbacks. We learn from failures and use them as stepping stones toward success.

13. **Enhancing Emotional Intelligence:** Managing change effectively requires emotional intelligence. Embracing change enhances our ability to regulate emotions,

empathize with others, and maintain composure in challenging situations.

14. **Expanding Perspectives:** Embracing change exposes us to diverse perspectives and cultures. This exposure broadens our understanding of the world and enhances our ability to collaborate with people from different backgrounds.

15. **Personal Growth and Fulfillment:** Ultimately, embracing change leads to personal growth and fulfillment. As we adapt, evolve, and seize new opportunities, we create a life that is rich in experiences and aligned with our true potential.

In conclusion, embracing change unlocks a world of growth and new opportunities. It strengthens our adaptability, fuels innovation, and helps us discover our inner strengths. By stepping out of our comfort zones, we break free from limiting beliefs and embrace the possibilities that change brings. Embracing change not only propels us forward in our personal and professional lives but also enriches our journey with a sense of fulfillment and purpose.

ACCEPTANCE AND ADAPTABILITY AS TOOLS FOR NAVIGATING LIFE'S UPS AND DOWNS

Acceptance and adaptability are invaluable tools for navigating life's ups and downs with resilience and grace. Let's explore how to cultivate these qualities:

1. **Practice Mindfulness:** Mindfulness involves staying present and aware of

your thoughts and emotions without judgment. By practicing mindfulness, you can observe life's changes without becoming overly attached or reactive.

2. **Embrace Impermanence:** Recognize that change is a natural part of life. Embracing the impermanence of situations and experiences helps you avoid resistance and allows you to flow with life's fluctuations.

3. **Develop Self-Awareness:** Understand your strengths, weaknesses, and triggers. Self-awareness helps you identify areas where you may struggle with acceptance or adaptability, enabling you to work on them intentionally.

4. **Reframe Challenges:** View challenges as opportunities for growth rather than as insurmountable obstacles. By reframing

your perspective, you can approach difficulties with a positive and proactive mindset.

5. **Cultivate Flexibility:** Be open to different possibilities and outcomes. Cultivating flexibility allows you to adjust your approach and expectations when circumstances change.

6. **Let Go of Control:** Understand that some situations are beyond your control. Learning to let go of the need to control every aspect of life reduces stress and allows you to focus on what you can influence.

7. **Practice Gratitude:** Cultivate gratitude for both the highs and lows of life. Gratitude helps you find meaning and appreciation even in challenging circumstances.

8. **Learn from Setbacks:** When faced with setbacks, view them as learning opportunities. Analyze what you can glean from the experience and how you can grow stronger as a result.

9. **Build a Support Network:** Surround yourself with supportive and understanding individuals. A strong support network can provide comfort and encouragement during difficult times.

10. **Set Realistic Expectations:** Set realistic and achievable goals for yourself. Unrealistic expectations can lead to disappointment and frustration, hindering your ability to adapt to changing situations.

11. **Practice Self-Compassion:** Be kind and understanding toward yourself during challenging times. Self-compassion allows

you to navigate setbacks with a sense of gentleness and understanding.

12. **Focus on Solutions:** Instead of dwelling on problems, direct your energy toward finding solutions. An adaptable mindset allows you to explore different avenues and consider creative approaches.

13. **Learn to Say No:** Know your limits and prioritize your well-being. Learning to say no to commitments that overwhelm you helps maintain balance and adapt to changing demands.

14. **Stay Grounded in Core Values:** Your core values provide a stable foundation during times of change. Staying grounded in your values helps you make decisions aligned with your authentic self.

15. **Celebrate Resilience:** Acknowledge and celebrate your resilience in overcoming

life's challenges. Celebrating your adaptability reinforces these positive qualities for future endeavors.

By incorporating acceptance and adaptability into your mindset and daily life, you equip yourself with powerful tools to navigate life's unpredictable journey. Embrace change with an open heart, and approach each experience as an opportunity for growth and learning.

As you cultivate acceptance and adaptability, you'll find that you can navigate life's ups and downs with greater ease, finding strength and wisdom in the face of adversity.

PRACTICAL EXERCISES AND INSIGHTFUL REFLECTIONS

1. **Mindful Breathing:** Practice a simple mindful breathing exercise to anchor yourself in the present moment. Take a few minutes each day to focus solely on your breath, observing its rhythm and feeling the sensation of each inhale and exhale. Use this exercise as a reminder that change is constant, and the breath symbolizes the ebb and flow of life.

Insightful Reflection: How does it feel to be fully present and attuned to your breath? What insights can you draw from this practice about the impermanence of each moment?

2. **The Seasons of Life:** Take a nature walk or spend time in a park, observing the

changing seasons. Reflect on the beauty of this cyclical transformation. Consider how the changing seasons mirror the stages of life and the impermanence of all things.

Insightful Reflection: How can you embrace the wisdom of nature's seasons and apply it to your own life's journey? What new possibilities emerge when you see life's changes as part of a natural and transformative cycle?

3. **Letter to Your Future Self:** Write a letter to your future self, imagining where you might be in one year or five years. Embrace the uncertainty of the future and share your hopes and aspirations, knowing that circumstances will inevitably change.

Insightful Reflection: How does writing this letter make you feel about the unknown future?

What fears and excitement arise, and how can you harness these emotions to embrace change and impermanence with courage?

4. **The Art of Letting Go:** Declutter a space in your home or workspace. As you sort through your belongings, contemplate the act of letting go of material possessions. Consider how letting go can create space for new experiences and opportunities.

Insightful Reflection: How does decluttering and letting go of material possessions translate to embracing change in other aspects of your life? What emotions arise during this process, and how can you apply this practice to emotional attachments as well?

5. **Facing Fears Head-On:** Identify a fear or change you have been avoiding. Take

small, deliberate steps to confront it, gradually desensitizing yourself to the discomfort. Journal your progress and acknowledge the growth that comes from facing fears.

Insightful Reflection: What insights did you gain from facing your fear? How did this experience reinforce the idea that embracing change and stepping into the unknown can lead to personal growth and transformation?

6. **Gratitude Journaling:** Keep a gratitude journal and write down three things you are grateful for each day. Embrace the impermanence of life's joys and challenges while cultivating an attitude of appreciation.

Insightful Reflection: How has practicing gratitude influenced your perception of change and impermanence? How can you continue to find gratitude amidst life's fluctuations?

7. **Circle of Support:** Reach out to your circle of support, whether friends, family, or mentors. Share your thoughts on embracing change and impermanence, and engage in a meaningful conversation about their experiences and insights.

Insightful Reflection: What wisdom and support do you gain from connecting with your circle of support? How can their perspectives deepen your understanding of change and inspire you to navigate life's ups and downs with greater resilience?

By incorporating these practical exercises and insightful reflections into your life, you will engage actively with the concept of embracing change and impermanence. These exercises not only resonate on a personal level but also bring the message to life, making the chapter a transformative and empowering experience for readers. So transform your life with these practical exercises and insightful reflections

CHAPTER 7

FINDING LIBERATION THROUGH GRATITUDE

Introduction

Welcome to Chapter 7: "Finding Liberation through Gratitude," where we embark on a journey of profound transformation and empowerment through the simple act of gratitude.

In this chapter, we delve into the extraordinary power of gratitude to liberate our minds and hearts from the burdens of negativity and discontent. Just as a single candle can illuminate an entire room, gratitude has the power to illuminate our lives, illuminating the path to joy, fulfillment, and abundance.

Join us as we explore the science and philosophy of gratitude, unveiling how this transformative practice rewires our brains, enhances our well-being, and strengthens our relationships.

Prepare to be captivated by the enlightening insights within these pages as we unlock the door to a world of liberation and abundance through the practice of gratitude.

Are you ready to embrace the liberating force of gratitude and unlock the secret to living a life of profound fulfillment? Let's embark on this captivating exploration together.

THE POWER OF GRATITUDE IN SHIFTING OUR PERSPECTIVES AND ATTITUDES

The power of gratitude lies in its profound ability to shift our perspectives and attitudes, transforming how we perceive and interact with the world around us. Gratitude is more than just saying "thank you"; it is a mindset, a practice, and a way of being that can lead to significant positive changes in our lives. Let's explore in-depth how gratitude has the power to shift our perspectives and attitudes:

1. **Focus on Abundance:** Gratitude redirects your focus from what you lack to what you have. Instead of dwelling on what is missing in your life, you must appreciate the abundance of blessings, big and small, that surround you daily.

2. **Cultivating Positivity:** Practicing gratitude encourages us to see the good even in challenging situations. By acknowledging the positive aspects of your life, you cultivate a more positive outlook on life.

3. **Reducing Negativity:** Gratitude acts as a natural antidote to negativity. When you regularly count your blessings, it becomes challenging for negativity to take root in your mind.

4. **Enhancing Resilience:** Gratitude fosters resilience by helping us reframe adversity. It allows you to find valuable lessons and silver linings in difficult experiences, making you more equipped to handle future challenges.

5. **Mindfulness and Presence:** Gratitude anchors you in the present moment. As we

become more aware of the things we are grateful for, we learn to savor and appreciate the richness of each moment.

6. **Strengthening Relationships:** Expressing gratitude to others strengthens our relationships and fosters a sense of connection. Gratitude helps you recognize and value the kindness and support you receive from those around you.

7. **Rewiring the Brain:** The practice of gratitude triggers positive neuroplasticity, rewiring your brain to focus on positive experiences. It helps break patterns of negativity and fosters a more optimistic outlook.

8. **Boosting Emotional Well-Being:** Gratitude has been linked to improved emotional well-being. Regularly practicing gratitude reduces stress,

anxiety, and depression, promoting overall mental health.

9. **Promoting Empathy and Compassion:** Gratitude enhances our ability to empathize with others. When you recognize and appreciate the good in your life, you are more likely to extend kindness and compassion to others.

10. **Shifting from Scarcity to Abundance Mindset:** Gratitude replaces the scarcity mindset with an abundance mindset. Instead of feeling like there is never enough, we embrace a sense of fulfillment and contentment.

11. **Boosting Self-Esteem:** Gratitude boosts self-esteem by acknowledging our worth and accomplishments. It reminds us of our strengths and capabilities, fostering a positive self-image.

12. **Increasing Generosity:** Gratitude often inspires us to pay it forward. When we receive kindness and generosity, we are more inclined to extend the same to others, creating a ripple effect of positivity.

13. **Finding Meaning and Purpose:** Gratitude helps you find meaning and purpose in your life. As you appreciate the value of each experience, you gain a deeper understanding of your life's journey.

14. **Altering the Perception of Time:** Gratitude alters your perception of time. When you focus on the positive aspects of life, time seems to slow down, allowing us to savor moments with greater depth.

15. **Creating a Virtuous Cycle:** As gratitude positively impacts our attitudes and

perspectives, it creates a virtuous cycle of positivity. The more we practice gratitude, the more positive changes we experience, reinforcing the practice.

In conclusion, the power of gratitude is transformative and far-reaching. By shifting our perspectives and attitudes, gratitude helps us see the world with fresh eyes, appreciate the beauty in every experience, and cultivate a profound sense of contentment and joy. As we embrace gratitude as a way of life, we unlock the door to a more fulfilling and abundant existence, nurturing a deep appreciation for the countless blessings that surround us each day.

ENCOURAGING GRATITUDE

Encouraging the practice of gratitude as a means of experiencing freedom and contentment is like opening the door to a world of profound fulfillment and joy. Gratitude acts as a powerful catalyst that transforms how we perceive and engage with life, liberating us from the shackles of negativity and discontent. Let's delve vividly into how the practice of gratitude fosters freedom and contentment:

1. **The Freedom of Perspective:** Gratitude liberates you from the constraints of a negative mindset. Instead of focusing on what is lacking or what went wrong, gratitude allows you to shift your perspective and appreciate the abundance of blessings that surround you.

   This freedom of perspective opens your heart to see the beauty and potential in every experience.

2. **Embracing the Present Moment:** Gratitude anchors you in the present moment. As you cultivate the habit of appreciating what you have here and now, you become less preoccupied with regrets of the past or worries about the future.

   This presence in the moment grants you the freedom to fully immerse yourself in the richness of life's offerings.

3. **Contentment in the Now:** By acknowledging and savoring the goodness in your life, gratitude cultivates contentment in the present. You learn to find joy and fulfillment in the simple pleasures and experiences that make up your daily existence.

This contentment becomes a source of inner freedom, as you recognize that happiness is not solely dependent on external circumstances.

4. **Letting Go of Comparison:** Gratitude encourages you to focus on your unique blessings, freeing you from the trap of constant comparison. When you appreciate your journey and the gifts you have, you no longer feel the need to measure yourself against others.

This liberation from comparison allows you to embrace your authenticity and walk your path with confidence.

5. **The Power of Gratitude Journaling:** Gratitude journaling is a practice that magnifies the experience of freedom and

contentment. As you write down the things you are grateful for, you capture the positive moments that may have otherwise slipped by unnoticed. This practice deepens your sense of appreciation and instills a lasting sense of contentment in your heart.

6. **Gratitude for Lessons in Adversity:** Gratitude empowers you to find meaning and growth in challenging times. When you express gratitude for the lessons learned during adversity, you experience a sense of freedom from bitterness and resentment.

This newfound wisdom becomes a source of contentment, knowing that every experience contributes to our growth.

7. **Freedom from the Need for More:** Gratitude helps you recognize the abundance that already exists in your life. You become less attached to the constant pursuit of external possessions or achievements as sources of happiness. This freedom from the need for more leads to contentment with what you have.

8. **Strength in Resilience:** Gratitude strengthens your resilience in the face of life's uncertainties. When you focus on the blessings and support you receive, you find the strength to navigate challenges with grace.

This resilience brings contentment, knowing that you have the inner resources to face whatever comes our way.

9. **Liberation from Materialism:** Gratitude invites you to place greater value on experiences, relationships, and intangible qualities rather than material possessions. This liberation from materialism fosters contentment in the richness of life's non-material gifts.

10. **Radiating Joy to Others:** The practice of gratitude allows you to share your joy and appreciation with others. As you express gratitude and kindness, you contribute to a positive and uplifting environment that nourishes your own sense of freedom and contentment.

In conclusion, encouraging the practice of gratitude unlocks the keys to experiencing freedom and contentment. Gratitude is a transformative force that liberates us from negative thought patterns and invites us to embrace the beauty of life's blessings. Through gratitude, we find contentment in the present moment and cultivate resilience in the face of challenges. It guides us to value the intangible treasures of life, fostering a deep sense of fulfillment and joy. Embrace gratitude as a way of life, and you will discover the boundless freedom and contentment that lie within your heart.

Daily gratitude exercises to cultivate a grateful mindset

Cultivating a grateful mindset involves incorporating gratitude exercises into your daily routine. Here are several daily gratitude exercises to help you embrace a grateful outlook on life:

1. **Gratitude Journaling:** Set aside a few minutes each morning or evening to write down three to five things you are grateful for. Reflect on the positive experiences, relationships, or moments that brought you joy during the day.

2. **Morning Gratitude Affirmations:** Begin your day with gratitude affirmations. As you wake up, say aloud or silently repeat affirmations like "I am grateful for the opportunities that today will bring" or "I am thankful for the people who enrich my life."

3. **Gratitude Walk:** During a walk outdoors, focus on the beauty around you. Notice the colors of the sky, the chirping of birds, or the feeling of the breeze. Express gratitude for the natural world and its wonders.

4. **Gratitude Jar:** Keep a jar or container in a visible place and fill it with notes of gratitude throughout the day. Whenever you feel grateful for something, jot it down on a piece of paper and add it to the jar.

5. **Gratitude Meditation:** Practice a gratitude meditation before bedtime. Close your eyes and focus on the things you are thankful for. Let gratitude fill your heart as you breathe deeply and embrace the feelings of appreciation.

6. **Random Acts of Kindness:** Perform one or more random acts of kindness each day. Whether it's a compliment, a smile, or an act of service, show appreciation to others and notice the positive impact it has on them and yourself.

7. **Gratitude Email:** Send a gratitude email or message to someone you appreciate. Express your thanks and let them know how much they mean to you.

8. **Gratitude Collage:** Create a gratitude collage with images or quotes that represent the things you are grateful for. Display it in a place where you can see it regularly.

9. **Mealtime Gratitude:** Before eating, take a moment to express gratitude for the food on your plate, the hands that prepared it, and the nourishment it provides.

10. **Gratitude Reflections:** Throughout the day, pause for a moment of reflection and find something to be grateful for in each situation, whether it's a challenge that taught you a lesson or a moment of joy.

11. **Gratitude Jar for Others:** Set up a separate gratitude jar or journal dedicated to acknowledging the kind acts or positive qualities of others. Write down moments when someone else made you feel grateful or touched your life positively.

12. **Gratitude Apps:** Use gratitude apps or online platforms that provide daily prompts and reminders to practice gratitude regularly.

13. **Gratitude Circle:** Gather with friends or family and take turns sharing something you are grateful for. Allow each person to feel the warmth of appreciation and connection.

14. **Gratitude Reminder:** Set a daily reminder on your phone or computer to pause for a moment and reflect on something you are grateful for.

15. **Gratitude Prayer or Blessing:** Incorporate a gratitude prayer or blessing into your morning, afternoon or evening routine to express thanks for the blessings in your life.

Remember, consistency is key to cultivating a grateful mindset. Choose the gratitude exercises that resonate with you the most and make them a part of your daily practice. Over time, you'll find that gratitude becomes a natural and uplifting way of approaching life's experiences.

CONCLUSION

As you reach the end of this book you stand at the threshold of a transformative journey. Throughout this captivating exploration, you have discovered the profound power of letting go, finding liberation in the act of surrender, and unlocking the boundless potential of a grateful heart. Now, let us take a moment to reflect on the key lessons that have paved the way for a more fulfilled and empowered life.

1. **The Art of Surrender:** You have learned that surrender does not signify weakness but strength. It is the act of releasing the tight grip on the steering wheel of life, trusting that you can be happy if you let yourself.

Through surrender, you free yourself from the burden of control and allow life to unfold in its divine timing.

2. **Embracing Change and Impermanence:** The inevitability of change and impermanence has been illuminated as a natural and transformative force. By embracing change, you cultivate adaptability and resilience, discovering the beauty in life's ever-shifting tides.

3. **The Power of Gratitude:** Gratitude has emerged as a profound catalyst for shifting perspectives and attitudes. It liberates you from negativity, anchors you in the present moment, and fosters contentment in life's abundance.

Through gratitude, you find joy in the simplest of blessings and discover a wealth of fulfillment within your heart.

As you bid farewell to these pages, I urge you to embark on this journey of letting go with open arms and a courageous heart. Embrace the freedom that comes from relinquishing the need for control and the beauty of living in harmony with the flow of life.

As you navigate the challenges and uncertainties that lay ahead, remember that letting go is not a one-time act but a continuous practice of growth and self-discovery.

Let each sunrise be a reminder that life offers you new opportunities to surrender, embrace change, and express gratitude. Embrace the wisdom that comes with facing fears, releasing past hurts, and detaching from outcomes.

Through each chapter, you will uncover the strength within you to break free from limiting beliefs, nurture trust in yourself and others, and find peace in the beauty of impermanence.

You are now equipped with the tools to sculpt a life of fulfillment and empowerment. Embrace this newfound freedom with unwavering hope and determination. Your journey of letting go will open doors to possibilities you never knew existed, and your heart will overflow with the abundance that comes from a grateful soul.

Go forth and live a life that echoes with the harmony of letting go. With every step, may your path be illuminated by the light of surrender, and may you inspire others to embark on their own quest for liberation and self-discovery.

As you turn the final page, I invite you to share your thoughts and experiences in a heartfelt review on Amazon. Your words have the power to touch the hearts of countless others, guiding them towards their own path of freedom and fulfillment.

May your heart be filled with gratitude for the journey you've undertaken, and may the light of letting go shine brightly within you forevermore. The world awaits your embrace of freedom, and I have no doubt that you will soar to unimaginable heights as you let go and let life work its magic.

Thank you for being a part of this transformative journey. Now, go forth and let go, for the possibilities are endless, and the freedom to embrace life's wonders awaits you.

With deepest gratitude and warmest wishes,

I Booky

www.ingramcontent.com/pod-product-compliance
Lightning Source LLC
Chambersburg PA
CBHW070949260726
48661CB00003B/1193